PICK ME UP

Inspirations, Motivations & Unsolicited Advice

SEPTEMBER 1, 2021
BY LALONNIE TRAVENIA
ILLUSTRATIONS BY DERRICK VAUGHN

And here we go...

(Mountain)

Everyday is an opportunity to do something different.

You can't get better if you don't get started.

Pray over your goals to give them power and remind you to walk the path to manifest them.

Be intentional.

(Coming Together)

Your lack of ambition cannot be my reality.

You cannot advance in what you do not pursue.

I control my time.

It's either all going to fall apart or it is going to work out. Either way, keep getting back up!

(More Than Before)

Stop overthinking and just do it.

There is not another you and there never will be. That by itself makes you pretty awesome to me.

Don't wait! Don't save it! Don't hold off! Now is as good a time as any.

NOW is a good time to have a good look and create a good day with a great attitude.

There is a time to work and a time to wait. Work until it's time to wait! **#HustleHard**

How many opportunities have you missed because you were waiting? And did what you were waiting for ever come through?

The biggest obstacle to my success has not been procrastination, it has been organization. I should start there! **#GetOrganized**

Restrictions and requirements are just suggestions. **#GoForIt #LetThemTellYouNo**

(Duet)

One day or Day one... you decide.

You have to make *me* time and not wait for it. If you wait for it, it may never come.

Allow yourself to remove your cape and be human sometimes.

Your parents either did their best or did nothing at all. At some point in your adulthood, you become the author of your life and are solely responsible for your actions and choices.

Always give others the forgiveness you'd seek.

(All In Her Own)

If someone asks how you are doing, tell them! You'll either get access to the help or support that you need or you will start the process of dealing with it by getting it off your chest. Win either way.

Secrets are decisions, not obligations. Know when to hold them and know when to let them go.

Smiles are free but frowns cost you joy. Stop robbing yourself, especially on someone else's behalf.

(Frustrations 1)

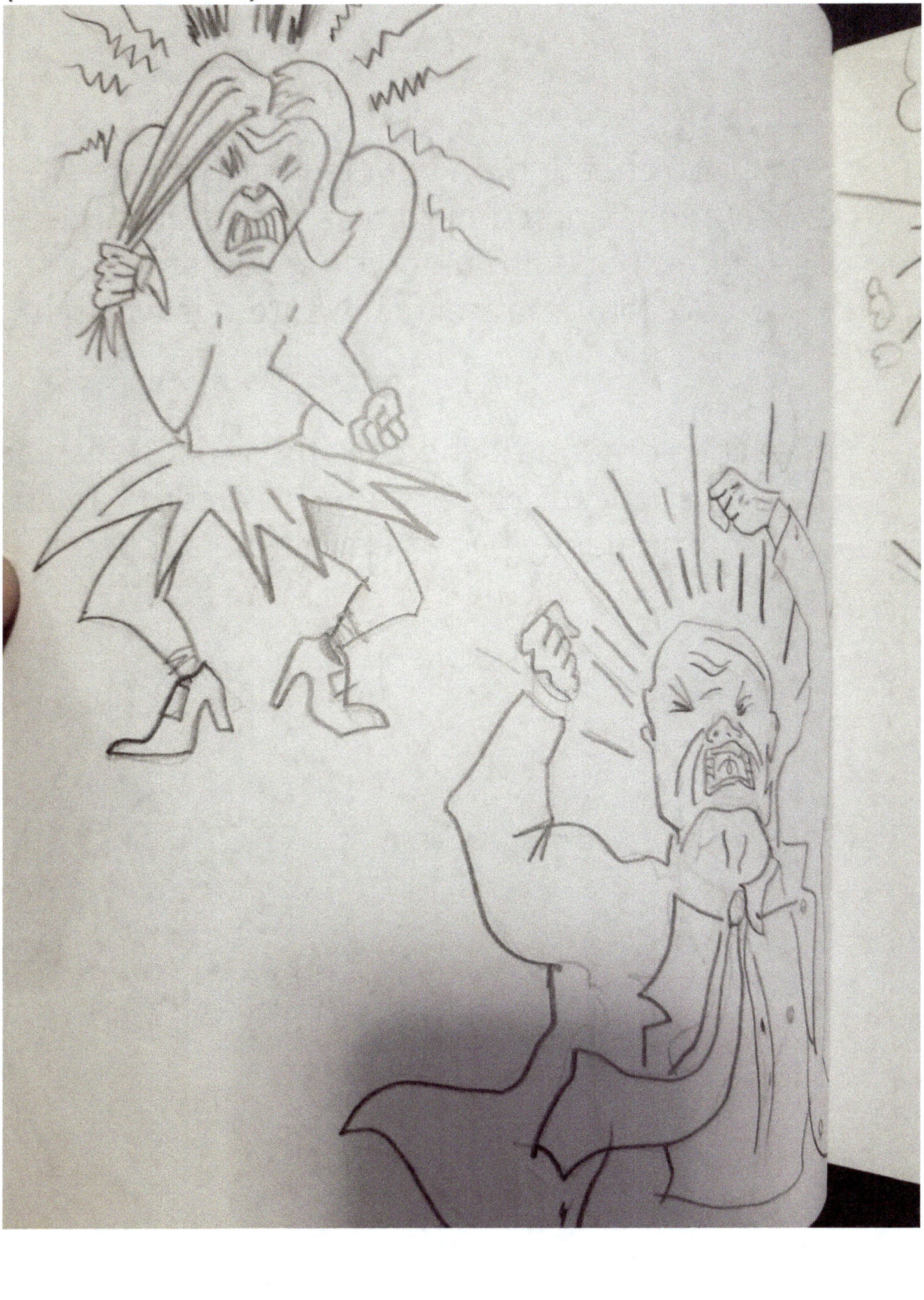

Stop cheating on yourself with lowered expectations and compromise. How can someone else learn to be faithful to you if you aren't? And if you do compromise, make sure it is worth it!

Stealing someone's choice is the most selfish act I've experienced. Stolen choice is a crime against humanity! Don't be that person!
#KarmaAlwaysComes

(Equally Yoking)

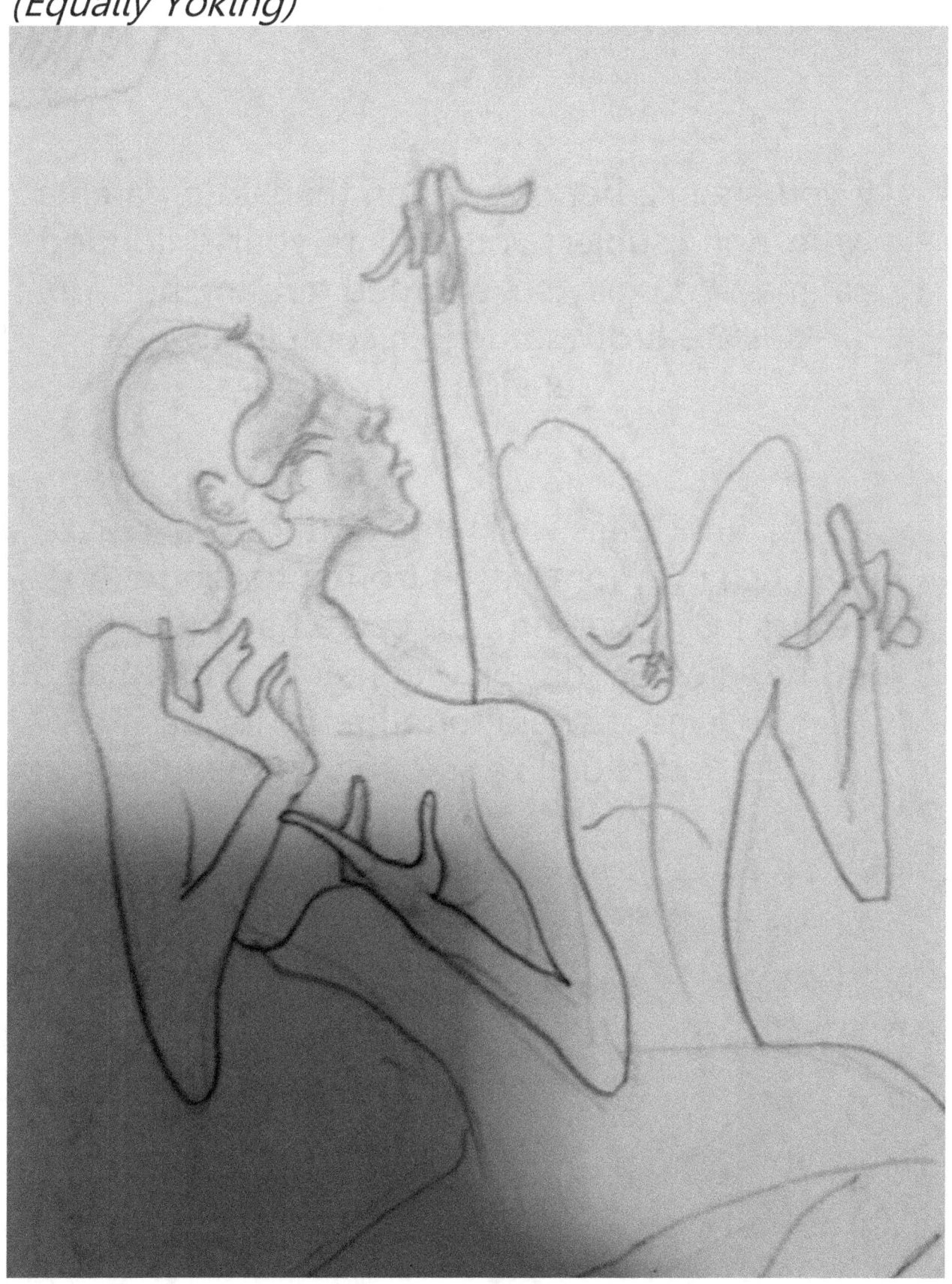

If you are in a better position than your parents were, don't subject your kids to your childhood traumas. You may have turned out fine but your kids are growing up in a completely new environment.

It took until I was well into adulthood to realize how much my mom wasn't born into motherhood. She was just a woman who had a baby. She didn't get the same handbook that I didn't. Funny, all of our lives are held together by love and determination like spit and bubblegum!

Use your job, not people.

(Family)

Notes and Doodles

Notes and Doodles

Being you is the easiest job that people complicate.

That's not true about you, so stop trying to prove it.

Sitting in silence can be as powerful as great advice.

If you wake up in the middle of the night and can't go back to sleep, that could be the universe showing you the time to do that thing you keep saying you don't have time to do.

(Maintaining the Village)

Imagine your hard day on someone else... now how easy is it to just smile and say hello?

We need to use words better. **#ManifestWhatYouSpeak**

Shorten the distance between I will and I am going to. The goal is "I'm done." **#Complete**

Kicking yourself for a year won't change the fact that now is still available. **#GetItDone**

Want different? Think different + Do different = CHANGE.

(Key)

You are perfect for the purpose that chose you.

You have value, even if you think no one sees it.

It'll be there when you get back.

Don't create or maintain relationships based on your assumptions. Facts and honesty build strong foundations.

Although life is only one shot, it comes with many do overs...take advantage when you can!

There is always room for coaching, but I am good at what I do.

If you can give your job 8 hours on a bad day, you can muster that same push to give your business or passion at least 3. Don't short yourself.

Honor your commitments; especially the ones to yourself.

(Relay)

Don't do anything out of anger; that is when some of the biggest mistakes happen.

Check with the source before you form your opinion or share information or risk being guilty of spreading gossip.

The only truly reliable source is a first-hand account.

People who hate on doers are probably donters.

Emotions don't always support facts. Remember that when receiving and delivering information about someone.

(Let's Jam)

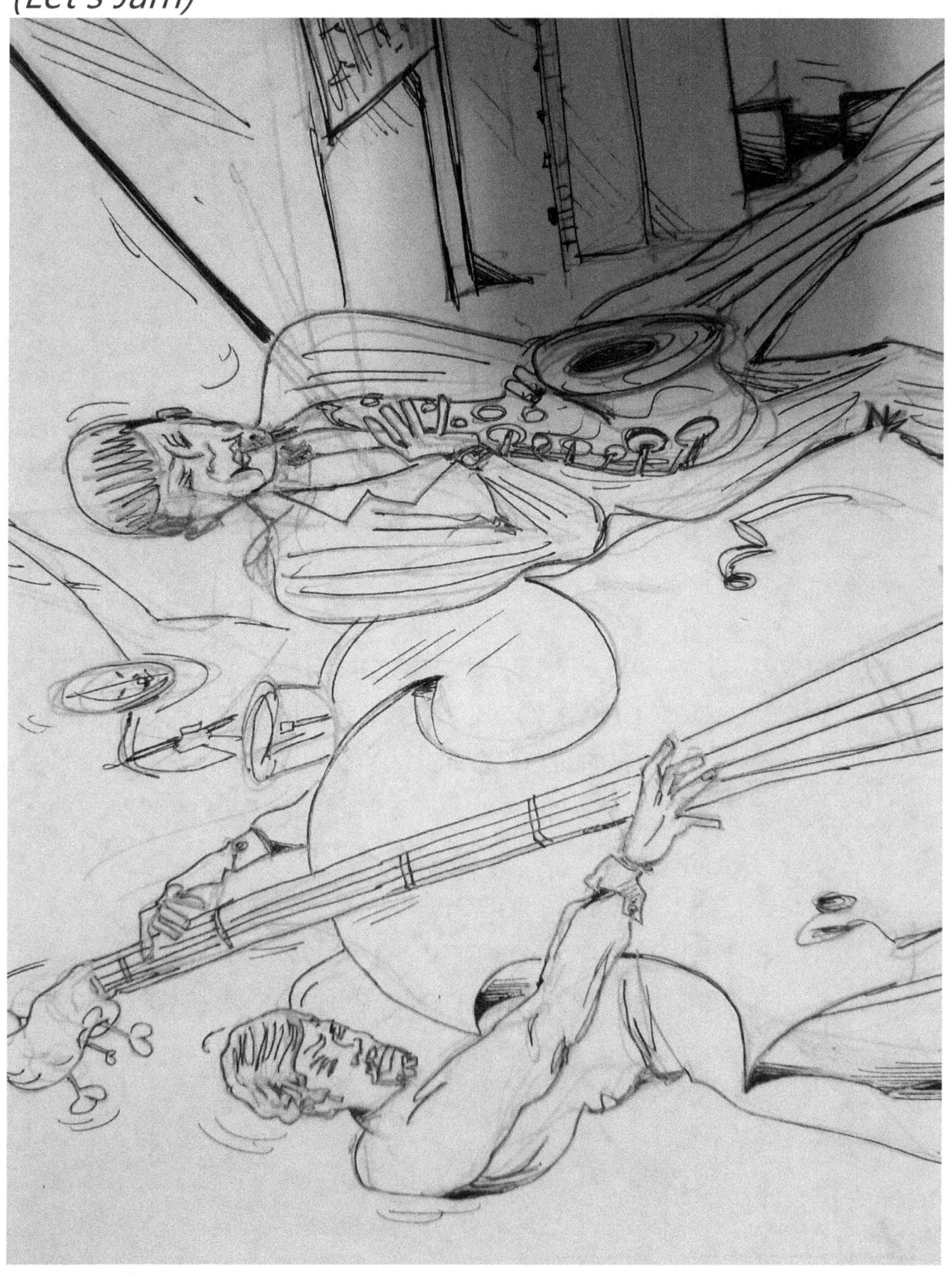

Jumping to conclusions is not a viable form of exercise.

I'll never be with someone I have to check up on, check-a-bitch over, or check in to...where there is healthy communication and mutual respect this is just part of the relationship.

Not loving yourself renders you incapable of truly loving a partner. Don't short yourself by giving someone half of you.

If you truly love someone your attraction may change and attention may shift but your honesty won't let you hurt them more than is needed to go in a new direction.

(Poised)

Not sure if something is "your thing"? Try it until you are. **#DontGiveUp**

Change your life one habit at a time.

Even a free spirit checks the date from time to time.

Shifting your energy may be easier than changing a habit. Do what works for you.

(Chess)

A baby doesn't stop a BOSS. A baby *never* stopped a BOSS. A BOSS makes moves, not excuses.

You might hurt my feelings a thousand times but you will only betray me once.

"I'm sorry" isn't always an admission of guilt; sometimes it is an act of compassion.

(She Ready)

Notes and Doodles

Notes and Doodles